Quick Knits

Written by Judy Ann Sadler
Illustrated by Esperança Melo

KIDS CAN PRESS

To Carly, who knits goodness and love into everything she does.

A very heartfelt thank you to Janet Filipchuk and all her lovely staff at London Yarns for so patiently answering all my questions.

Text © 2006 Judy Ann Sadler
Illustrations © 2006 Esperança Melo

KIDS CAN DO IT® and the 📖® logo are trademarks of Kids Can Press Ltd.

Kids Can Press acknowledges the financial support of the Government of Ontario, through the Ontario Media Development Corporation's Ontario Book Initiative, and the Government of Canada, through the BPIDP, for our publishing activity.

Published in Canada by
Kids Can Press Ltd.
29 Birch Avenue
Toronto, ON M4V 1E2

Published in the U.S. by
Kids Can Press Ltd.
2250 Military Road
Tonawanda, NY 14150

www.kidscanpress.com

Edited by Laurie Wark
Designed by Katie Collett
Photography by Ray Boudreau
Printed and bound in China

The hardcover edition of this book is smyth sewn casebound.
The paperback edition of this book is limp sewn with a drawn-on cover.

CM 06 0 9 8 7 6 5 4 3 2 1
CM PA 06 0 9 8 7 6 5 4 3 2 1

Library and Archives Canada Cataloguing in Publication

Sadler, Judy Ann, 1959–

Quick knits / written by Judy Ann Sadler ; illustrated by Esperança Melo.

(Kids can do it)

ISBN-13: 978-1-55337-963-8 (bound) ISBN-10: 1-55337-963-2 (bound)
ISBN-13: 978-1-55337-964-5 (pbk.) ISBN-10: 1-55337-964-0 (pbk.)

1. Knitting—Juvenile literature. 2. Knitting—Patterns—Juvenile literature. I. Melo, Esperança II. Title. III. Series.

TT820.S245 2006   j746.43'2   C2005-907023-4

Kids Can Press is a LORUS™ Entertainment company

Contents

Knit now!

Whether you're knitting for the first time or looking for some new quick-knit items, this book is for you! Most of the projects are made with big needles and thick yarn, so they are fast and easy to make. Follow the basics — casting on, knitting, purling and casting off — and you'll be knitting up a storm in no time. Start with a simple hat and scarf, then knit your way through the book to the backpack and sweater. You'll want to make two of everything: one for yourself and one for a friend! Soon you'll be part of a worldwide, ancient society of knitters whose skills have been handed down through many generations. Keep the knitting bug alive by setting up a knitting club to share ideas and tips, and show your not-yet-knitting friends how to get started.

Happy knitting!

YARN

The most common yarns are made from wool, cotton, acrylic and polyester. Novelty yarns are often a mixture of these fibers, and they'll give your knitted fabric interesting textures. Try long and short eyelash yarns, feathery acrylics, sparkling blends, soft chenille, fun fur and fine, washable merino wool. There are always fabulous new colors and types of yarn to use.

Keep your yarn labels in a notebook, along with a yarn sample and a photograph or description of what you made. Yarn labels list important information such as fiber content, washing instructions, yarn thickness, knitting gauge and dye lot. The dye lot is a number given by the manufacturer to a batch of yarn dyed at the same time. You should make your project using yarns from the same dye lot, so buy a little extra of each kind in case the store runs out of your dye lot. You can usually return unused balls of yarn to the store.

KNITTING NEEDLES

Knitting needles are sized in millimeters and by American standard numbers. They are made from many different materials, such as plastic, metal and wood, and come in different lengths. You will be using thick needles (6 mm [U.S. 9] or larger) for the projects in this book.

Use a needle gauge (a knitting ruler with holes in it) to figure out what size your needles are in case they are not marked in both millimeters and American sizes.

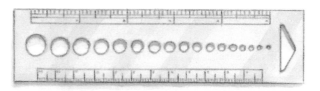

POINT PROTECTORS OR STOPPERS

These small rubber caps fit on the ends of your knitting needles. They keep the stitches on the needles and prevent the needles from poking through your knitting bag.

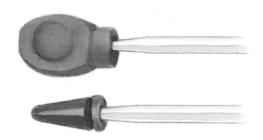

YARN NEEDLE

Yarn needles are also called craft, plastic canvas or knitters needles. They have a blunt tip and large eye. You'll need one to stitch seams in some of your knitted items.

WINDING YARN

Yarn often comes in a ball that is ready to use. It is best to pull the end of the yarn out from the center of the ball. If you pull out a clump of yarn along with it, that's okay. You will use it up quickly as you knit.

If your yarn comes in a skein, wind it into a ball before using it. Untie or cut the yarn that holds the skein together. Loop the bundle of yarn around the back of a chair or someone's hands or knees. Take one yarn end and wind it around two fingers about five times. Slide the yarn off your fingers and start loosely winding it into a ball. As you wind, keep turning the ball to make an even shape. When you are finished, tuck the end under a couple of strands of yarn, where you can easily get hold of it when you are ready to knit.

Casting on

Casting on means putting the first row of stitches on your needle.

1 Make a slipknot in the yarn, as shown. (The instructions for each project will tell you where on the yarn to make the knot.)

2 Pick up a needle in your right hand and rest your index finger along the needle. Put the slipknot on this needle so that the short end of the yarn is closest to you. Pull on the yarn ends so that the slipknot fits loosely on the needle.

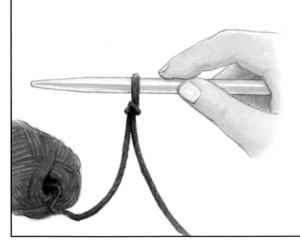

3 Put your left thumb and index finger between the two strands of yarn hanging down. Grasp both strands with the other three fingers on your left hand.

4 Spread apart your index finger and thumb. Turn your left hand so that your palm is toward you.

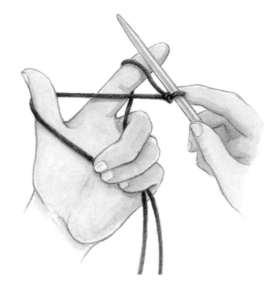

5 Keep the yarn tight as you dip the tip of the needle toward you, then up into the loop on your thumb.

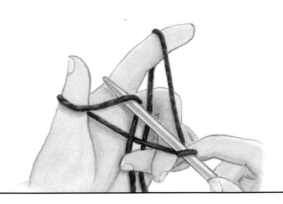

6 Turn your left hand so that your palm is facing sideways. Direct the tip of the needle toward your index finger and down into the center of the loop there to pick it up. Point the needle upward and turn your palm back toward you.

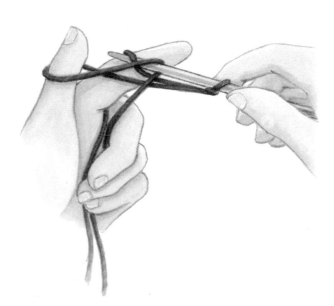

7 Direct the tip of the needle down into the center of the loop on your thumb and bring it out under the strand of yarn closest to you. Point the tip of the needle upward.

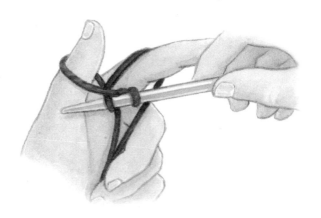

8 Allow the loop to slide off your thumb. Gently pull down on the strand and up with the needle to tighten the new stitch onto the needle. It should be closer to the tip of the needle than the slipknot is.

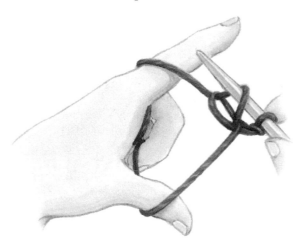

9 Repeat steps 4 to 8 until you have cast on all the stitches you need.

TIP

If you find it difficult to cast on loosely, try holding a size 5.5 or 6 mm (U.S. 9 or 10) needle along your large needle, so that the knob end is at the tip of the large needle. As you cast on, leave a bit of space between each stitch, then snug the stitch against both needles. When you are finished casting on, slide out the narrower needle.

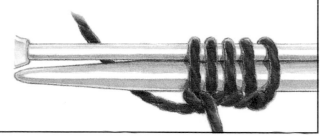

Knit stitch

To begin the knit stitch, you need a pair of knitting needles with stitches cast on one of them (page 6).

1 Hold the needle with the stitches on it in your left hand and the empty needle in your right hand. Slide the tip of the right needle up into the first stitch and push it behind the left needle to form an **X**.

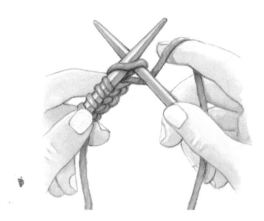

2 With your right hand, wind the working yarn (coming from the ball, not the leftover yarn tail) behind and around the right needle in a counterclockwise direction. The yarn should go between the needles.

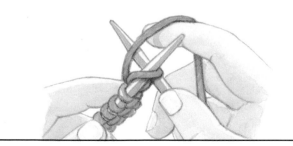

3 Dip the needle down and toward you so that it goes under and through the stitch on the left needle. The right needle should be in front of the left one and have one loop of yarn on it.

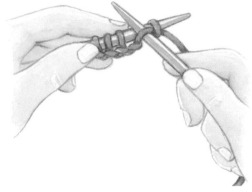

4 Slide the right needle upward so that the stitch comes off the left needle and stays on the right one. You have completed one knit stitch. The first stitch is the most difficult to knit because it sometimes gets big and loose. Keep it small by firmly holding onto the working yarn. After you knit the first stitch, pull on the working yarn so that the stitch is snug to your needle.

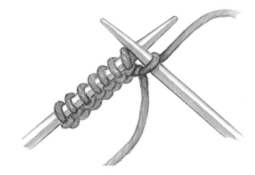

5 Finish the row by repeating steps 1 to 4, then move the full needle to your left hand to begin row 2.

Picking up stitches

To knit the earflaps onto the hat on page 24, you'll need to know how to pick up stitches.

1 Hold the knitted item with the good side facing you and the edge you are adding stitches to at the top.

2 Poke your right needle through a stitch at the edge (to the right of where you want to add stitches). Loop your working yarn around the needle. Fold the working yarn back on itself about 20 cm (8 in.) from the end.

3 Draw the loop toward you through the stitch, from the back to the front. You have now picked up one stitch.

4 For the second stitch, poke your needle into the next stitch to the left of the first one. Wrap both strands of yarn (the working yarn and the yarn tail) around the needle as if you are knitting it, and pull the loop through to the front.

5 Continue picking up stitches, working from right to left. After a few stitches, the tail will be woven in, so continue with just the working yarn.

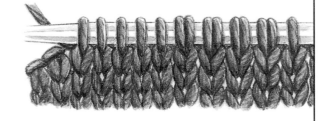

6 When you have all the stitches you need, move the full needle to your left hand. Knit the row if you are doing the garter stitch (page 11), and purl it if you are doing a stockinette stitch (page 11).

Purl stitch

Once you are comfortable with the knit stitch (page 8), the purl stitch is easy to do. To begin the purl stitch, you need a pair of knitting needles with stitches cast on one of them (page 6).

1 Hold the needle with the stitches on it in your left hand and the empty needle in your right hand.

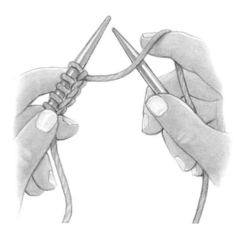

2 With the working yarn in the front, slide the empty needle into the first stitch so that the right needle is in front of the left needle.

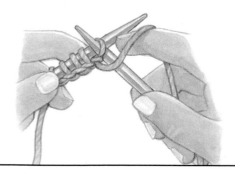

3 Use your right hand to wrap the working yarn around the right needle in a counter-clockwise direction.

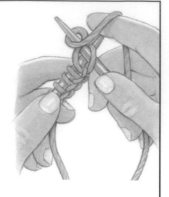

4 Hold the right needle and the yarn with your right hand. Don't let the yarn come off as you push the tip of this needle down through the stitch on the left needle. The right needle should be behind the left one and have one loop of yarn on it.

5 Lift up the right needle so that the stitch comes off the left needle and stays on the right one. You have now completed one purl stitch.

6 Finish the row by repeating steps 1 to 5, then move the full needle to your left hand and begin row 2.

Knitting stitches

Combine the basic stitches, knit and purl (pages 8 and 10), to create different kinds of knitted fabrics.

The garter stitch creates a bumpy knitted fabric that doesn't curl at the edges and looks the same on both sides. For the garter stitch, knit every stitch in every row.

The stockinette stitch (also known as the stocking stitch) makes a knitted fabric that curls at the edges. It's smooth on one side (the right side) and bumpy on the other (the wrong side). For the stockinette stitch, knit one row and purl the next.

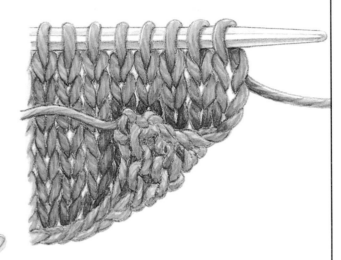

The seed stitch (also known as the moss stitch) makes a lovely, bumpy knitted fabric the same on both sides. For the seed stitch, cast on (page 6) an odd number of stitches. Knit the first stitch and purl the second. Knit and purl across each row, starting and ending with a knit stitch.

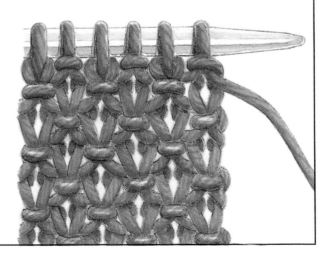

Increasing

For some projects, you will need to increase the number of stitches you are knitting per row to help shape your item. The project instructions tell you when you need to increase.

1 Begin a knit stitch as usual, by putting the right needle into a stitch on the left needle (step 1, page 8).

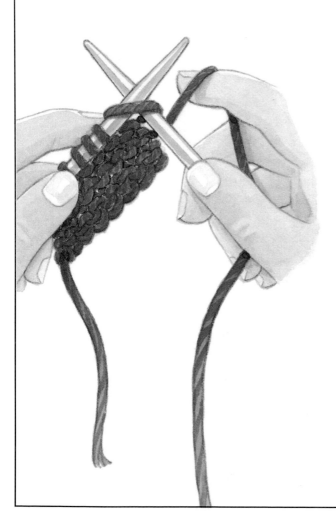

2 Knit the stitch (steps 2 and 3, page 8), but just before you slide it off the left needle, put the right needle into the back of the same stitch you just knit.

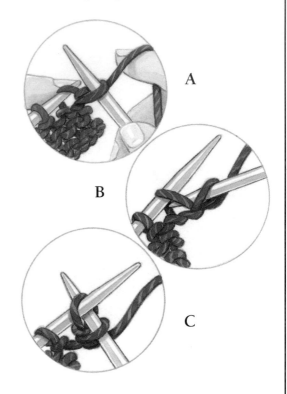

A

B

C

3 Knit the stitch again and slide the old stitch off the left needle. You will now have an extra stitch on the right needle. You've made two stitches out of one.

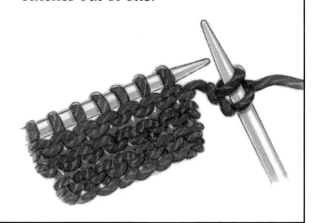

Decreasing

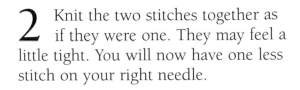

2 Knit the two stitches together as if they were one. They may feel a little tight. You will now have one less stitch on your right needle.

Sometimes you will need to decrease the number of stitches you are knitting to help shape your item.

1 Begin the knit stitch (page 8) as usual, but instead of putting the tip of your right needle into one stitch on the left needle, put it into two stitches.

Casting off

Casting off is also known as binding off. This is how you take the last row of stitches off the needle so that your knitting does not unravel.

1 Knit (page 8) the first two stitches onto the right needle as usual.

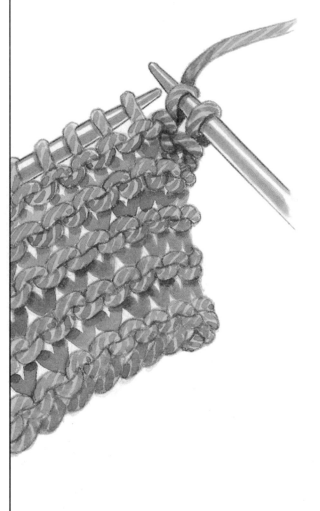

2 Use the left needle (or your fingers) to lift the first stitch (the one farthest from the tip) over the second one and off the end of the right needle.

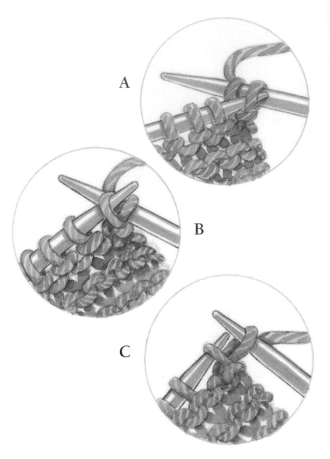

A

B

C

3 Knit the next stitch. Again, lift the first stitch over the second one and let it off the needle. Continue until there are no stitches on the left needle and just one on the right needle.

4 Cut the yarn, leaving a 20 cm (8 in.) tail. Pull gently on the last stitch to make it larger. Remove the knitting needle. Bring the yarn tail through the loop and pull it snug.

5 Use a yarn needle to weave in the yarn tail, then trim it off.

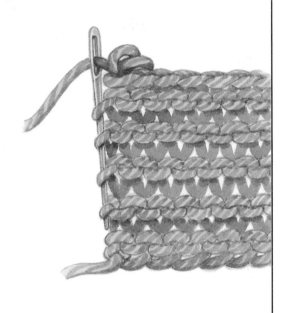

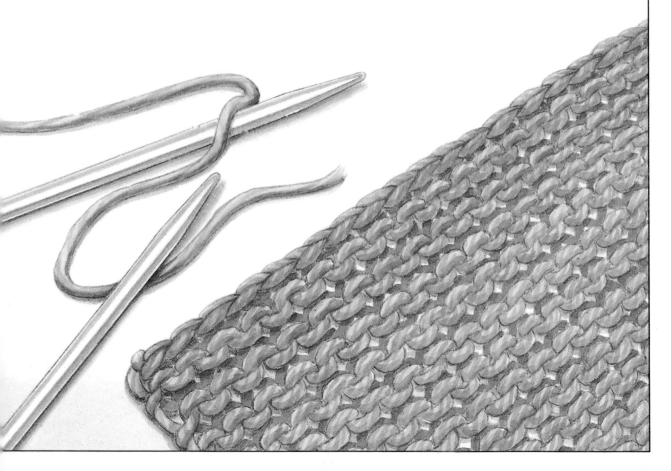

Fix it

It is best to catch mistakes early, so check your knitting often for holes. Also, check your needle for the correct number of stitches.

A common knitting mistake is to gain a stitch at the beginning of a row. When you are ready to knit the first stitch, make sure that the working yarn is hanging straight down, not over to the back. Otherwise, you will end up with an extra loop on your needle.

UNRAVEL STITCHES

You can carefully unravel your stitches one at a time by sliding them off the right needle, pulling gently on the working yarn and sliding the stitches back onto the left needle. Make sure that when you slip the stitches back onto the left needle, they are positioned as shown.

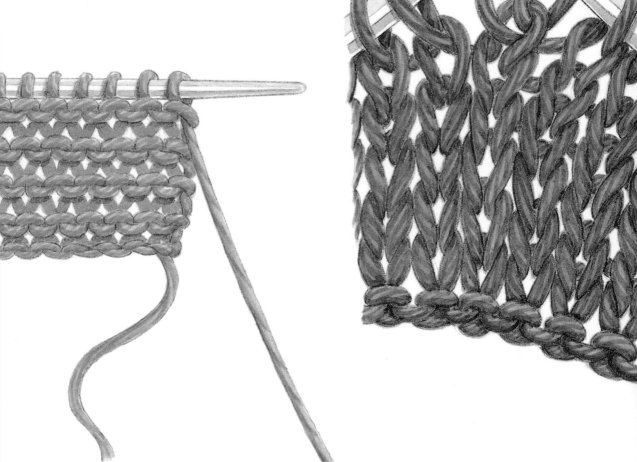

UNRAVEL ROWS

If you need to unravel a few rows, carefully slide the stitches off the full needle and start pulling gently on the working yarn. Make sure that when you slip the stitches back onto your needle, they are positioned as shown.

UNKNIT

If you realize partway through a row that you have made a mistake, poke the left needle into the stitch below the one you just made. Slide the stitch you just made off the right needle, pulling out the yarn as you go. You can unknit entire rows this way, too.

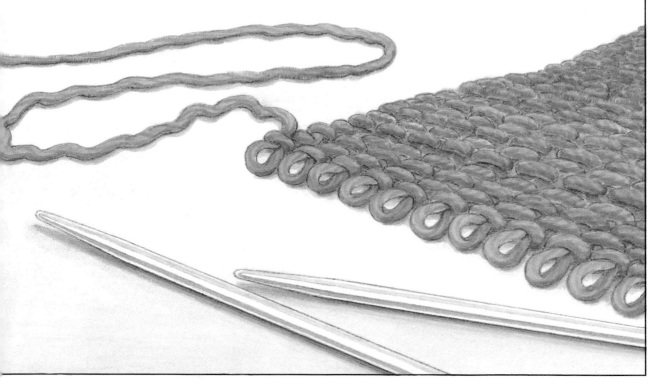

Sassy scarf

Once you've knitted this simple, fun scarf, you'll be hooked on knitting for life. Make yourself one in every color, and then knit some for your friends, too!

YOU WILL NEED

- about 60 m (65 yd.) of eyelash or other novelty yarn
- knitting needles, size 10 mm (U.S. 15)
- a ruler or measuring tape, scissors, a yarn needle

1 Make a slipknot about 50 cm (20 in.) from the end of the yarn. Cast on (page 6) 14 loose stitches.

2 Knit the first stitch (page 8). With novelty yarns, it can be tricky to see your stitches. As you knit the rest of the row, separate each stitch on the left needle to make sure that you knit one stitch at a time.

3 Keep knitting every stitch in every row (garter stitch, page 11) until your scarf is about 125 cm (50 in.) long.

4 Cast off (page 14). Use a yarn needle to weave the two yarn tails into the ends of your scarf.

5 To wear your scarf, fold it in half, wrap it around your neck and slip the two ends through the loop.

KNIT ON!

To make a fringe for your scarf, wrap yarn around the width of a book, or a piece of cardboard, about 15 cm (6 in.) wide about 60 times. Cut the yarn along one edge of the book. Fold three or four pieces of the cut yarn in half. Pull open a stitch at one corner of the scarf. Push the loop end of the folded yarn through the stitch and pull the yarn ends through the loop. Continue the fringe along both ends of the scarf.

To make a thick scarf, double up your yarn or combine different yarns. Try a very fine, feathery novelty yarn with a plain worsted weight or chunky yarn. Use both yarns at the same time, holding the two strands together as if they were one. Cast at least 8 stitches onto size 10 mm (U.S. 15) needles. Knit every stitch in every row until the scarf is the length you'd like. Cast off and weave in the yarn tails with a yarn needle.

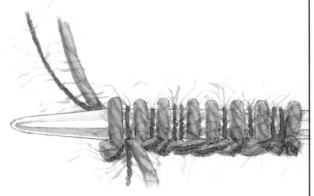

To make a wide, thick scarf, choose a soft bulky or super bulky weight yarn. Cast 16 to 20 stitches onto size 10 mm (U.S. 15) needles. Knit every stitch in every row until the scarf is the length you'd like. Cast off and weave in the yarn tails with a yarn needle.

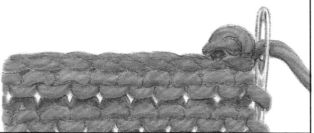

Crazy cuffs

Let your imagination go crazy knitting trim for your jeans, jacket, sweater, hat or whatever. Experiment with eyelash yarn, furry yarn, sparkling yarn or any novelty yarn you like.

YOU WILL NEED

- an item of clothing
- a ball of novelty yarn
- knitting needles, size 6 or 6.5 mm (U.S. 10 or 10½)
- a sturdy sewing needle and thread to match your yarn
- a ruler or measuring tape, scissors, a yarn needle

1 Measure around the area of clothing you want to trim, so that you know the length to knit.

2 Cast on (page 6) 7 to 10 stitches, depending on how wide you want the trim to be.

3 Knit (page 8) every stitch in every row (garter stitch, page 11) until the trim is the right length.

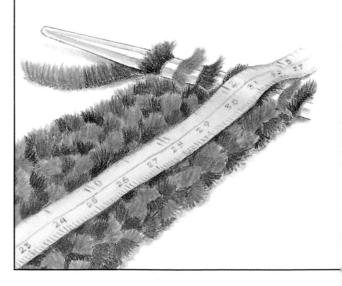

4 Cast off (page 14). Use a yarn needle to weave in the two yarn tails.

5 Knit any other pieces of trim you need.

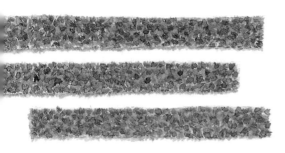

6 Cut a piece of thread about 60 cm (24 in.) long. Thread your sewing needle and pull the strands even. Knot them together at the ends.

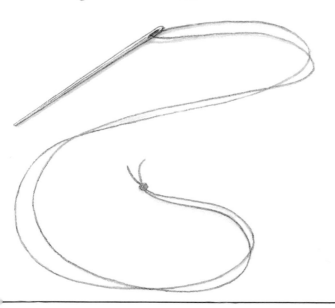

7 Push the needle up through the fabric where you want to stitch your trim and use a running stitch to sew it in place, as shown. When you run out of thread or reach the end, knot the thread and trim it.

KNIT ON!

● Knit crazy cuffs for the pillow on page 32, the slippers on page 34 or the sweater on page 36. Stitch the trim in place with yarn and a yarn needle.

Roll-rim hat

By using big needles and two strands of yarn together, you can knit up this hat in no time flat! Instead of using two types of yarn, you can also knit this hat using one strand of super bulky yarn.

YOU WILL NEED

- about 60 m (65 yd.) of chunky weight yarn, with a gauge of 12 to 15 stitches in 10 cm (4 in.)
- about 60 m (65 yd.) of knitting worsted weight yarn, with a gauge of 18 to 20 stitches in 10 cm (4 in.)
- knitting needles, size 10 mm (U.S. 15)
- a ruler or measuring tape, scissors, a yarn needle

1 Using both yarns at the same time, hold the two ends together as if they were one. Make a slipknot 190 cm (75 in.) from the end and cast on (page 6) 45 stitches.

2 To keep track of whether you should knit or purl a row, mark the empty needle with a short piece of yarn at the knob end. Knit (page 8) the first row. Now the stitches are on the marked needle. Purl (page 10) the second row. Keep knitting the rows when the stitches are on the unmarked needle and purling when they are on the marked needle.

3 Continue until you have 18 cm (7 in.) of stockinette stitch (page 11) and the stitches are on the unmarked needle (unroll the edge when you measure).

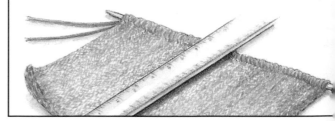

4 Begin to decrease (page 13) by knitting the first stitch, then knit the next 2 stitches together. Repeat the pattern (knit 1, then knit 2 together) across the whole row, ending with knitting 2 together. You should now have 30 stitches.

5 Purl all 30 stitches in the next row.

6 Decrease again by knitting 1, then knitting 2 together across the whole row, ending with knitting 2 together. You should now have 20 stitches.

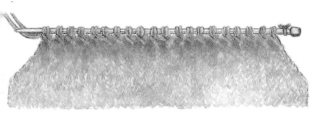

7 Purl all 20 stitches in the next row.

8 Knit 2 together across the last row so that you have 10 stitches left.

9 Cut the yarn, leaving a 75 cm (30 in.) tail. Thread it into the yarn needle. Slide the stitches, one at a time, from the knitting needle to the yarn needle and onto the yarn tail. Be sure to catch all the double loops.

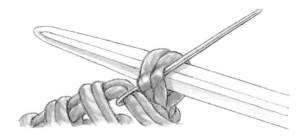

10 With the hat inside out, pull firmly on the yarn tail to gather the stitches into a tight circle. Using the yarn needle, stitch the circle closed, then stitch together the back of the hat taking a few stitches from each edge. When you get to the bottom, unroll it before you stitch the edges together.

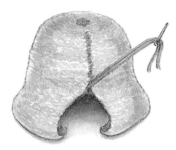

11 When you are finished, make a couple of stitches in the same spot, then weave in and trim the yarn tail. Weave in and trim the starting yarn tail, too.

Earflap hat

Add a fun tassel to this funky hat, and you'll never want to take the hat off!

YOU WILL NEED

- about 70 m (75 yd.) of chunky weight yarn, with a gauge of 12 to 15 stitches in 10 cm (4 in.)
- about 70 m (75 yd.) of knitting worsted weight yarn, with a gauge of 18 to 20 stitches in 10 cm (4 in.)
- knitting needles, size 10 mm (U.S. 15)
- a ruler or measuring tape, scissors, a yarn needle, pins

1 Using both yarns at the same time, hold the two ends together as if they were one. Make a slipknot 190 cm (75 in.) from the end and loosely cast on (page 6) 45 stitches.

2 Purl (page 10) the first two rows.

3 To keep track of whether you should knit or purl a row, mark the empty needle with a short piece of yarn at the knob end. Knit (page 8) the third row. Now the stitches are on the marked needle. Purl the fourth row. Knit the rows when the stitches are on the unmarked needle and purl when they are on the marked needle.

4 Continue until you have 15 cm (6 in.) of stockinette stitch (page 11) and the stitches are on the unmarked needle.

5 To decrease and finish, follow steps 4 to 11 on page 23.

6 To add earflaps, place the hat on a table with the seam at the left and the top of the hat closest to you. Put in a pin about 5 cm (2 in.) from the seam and another about 10 cm (4 in.) farther from the first.

7 Pick up (page 9) about 10 stitches between the pins. Remove the pins. Purl the next row, but to prevent the edges of the earflap from curling, knit the first and last stitch of this and each purl row as you stockinette stitch for the next 6 cm (2½ in.). End with a purl row.

8 Begin to decrease (page 13) by knitting 2 stitches together at the beginning and end of the next row. Purl the next row. Knit 2 together at the beginning and end of the following row. Purl the next row, and so on, until you have 2 or 3 stitches left. Knit those stitches together so that you have 1 stitch left.

9 Cut the working yarn, leaving a 75 cm (30 in.) tail. As you pull open the remaining stitch on your needle, the tail will shorten. Pull until the loop and the remaining length of the tail are even, snip the loop and braid the three strands together. Knot the end of the braid.

10 Turn the hat over so the seam is at the right. Repeat steps 6 to 9 to make the other earflap.

11 To finish your hat, cut at least nine pieces of yarn, each about 25 cm (10 in.) long. Knot them together at one end, braid them, then knot the other end. Poke one knotted end of the tassel into a stitch hole at the top of the hat, then stitch it in place.

Drawstring backpack

This backpack will hold all the essentials! Try combining yarns of different colors and textures.

YOU WILL NEED

- about 150 m (163 yd.) each of 2 balls of chunky weight yarn, each with a gauge of 12 to 14 stitches in 10 cm (4 in.)
- knitting needles, size 10 mm (U.S. 15)
- extra yarn for the drawstring
- a ruler or measuring tape, scissors, a yarn needle

1 Using both yarns at the same time, hold the two ends together as if they were one. Make a slipknot 150 cm (60 in.) from the end and cast on (page 6) 24 stitches. Do not trim the tail.

2 Knit (page 8) the first row.

3 In the second row, you will begin knitting a row of holes. Knit the first stitch, then make a "yarn over" (yo) by bringing the yarn forward between the needles. With the yarn still in front, knit the next 2 stitches together (they will feel tight). Knit the following stitch, then make another yarn over and knit the next 2 together. Continue this pattern across the row, ending with knitting the last 2 together. You should still have 24 stitches.

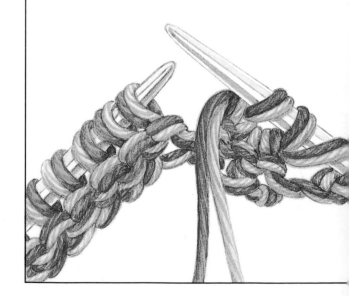

4 Knit every stitch in the next row. You will find that where you made a yarn over, the stitch is very loose. Knit it the same way as any other stitch. When you are finished knitting this row, you should have eight holes.

5 Knit every stitch in every row (garter stitch, page 11) until you have about 55 cm (22 in.) and the yarn tail is in the bottom right corner.

6 Make another row of holes by repeating steps 3 and 4.

7 Cast off (page 14), leaving a 75 cm (30 in.) tail.

8 Fold the knitting in half so that the rows of holes at each end are even. Thread the tails into a yarn needle and stitch the side seams. At the end of each seam, make a couple of stitches in the same spot, then weave in and trim the yarn tail.

9 To make the drawstring cord, cast on 4 stitches with one strand of yarn. Knit the first row and purl (page 10) the next. (If you find it tricky to knit the narrow cord on thick needles, you can use smaller needles.) Every once in a while as you knit and purl these short rows, stretch the cord taut so it curls. When it is about 125 to 150 cm (50 to 60 in.) long, cast off, leaving a 25 cm (10 in.) tail. Make another cord the same length.

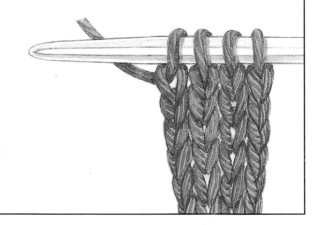

Instructions continue on the next page ☞

10 Beginning and ending at the right seam, weave one cord in and out of the holes you knitted around the top of the backpack. Tie the cord ends together with an overhand knot.

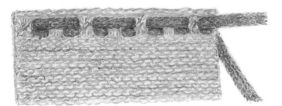

11 Beginning and ending at the left seam, weave the other cord in and out of the holes in the opposite way. Tie the cord ends together with an overhand knot.

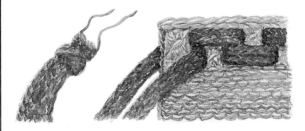

12 Thread the yarn tails at the end of one knotted cord into the yarn needle. Stitch the cord to the bottom corner. Stitch the other cord to the other bottom corner.

13 Pull the cords in opposite directions to close the bag.

KNIT ON!

● If you'd like the knitted fabric of your backpack to be thicker, try using thicker yarn or three strands of yarn.

● Instead of knitting a drawstring cord, use a thick braided cord.

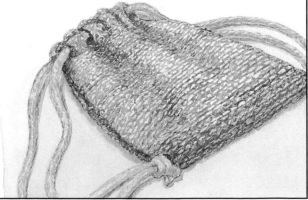

Wee wallet

After you've knitted a bunch of these wallets, check the "Knit on" ideas (page 31) for how to add a handle or to convert one into a cell phone cozy.

YOU WILL NEED

- about 20 m (22 yd.) of chunky weight yarn
- knitting needles, size 5.5 or 6 mm (U.S. 9 or 10)
- a button
- a sewing needle and thread to match your yarn
- a ruler or measuring tape, scissors, a yarn needle

1 Make a slipknot 45 cm (18 in.) from the end of the yarn. Cast on (page 6) 11 stitches. Mark the empty needle with a small piece of yarn at the knob end.

2 Knit (page 8) the first stitch. Bring the yarn to the front and purl (page 10) the second stitch. Bring the yarn to the back and knit the third stitch. Continue to knit and purl to the end of the row, bringing the yarn back and forth between stitches (seed stitch, page 11).

3 Seed stitch the rest of the rows, starting and ending with a knit stitch. If you get confused about whether to knit or purl, take a look at the next stitch on your left needle. If it looks like a **V** shape, purl that stitch. If it looks like a bump or tight loop, knit that stitch. Continue until you have about 20 cm (8 in.) and your stitches are on the unmarked needle.

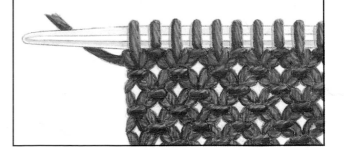

Instructions continue on the next page ☞

4 You will be knitting the flaps in the garter stitch (page 11). Begin to decrease (page 13) by knitting the first 2 stitches together. Knit the next 7 stitches, and then knit the last 2 together. You should have 9 stitches left.

6 Knit the first stitch, then the second in the next row. Make a "yarn over" (yo) by bringing the yarn forward between the needles. With the yarn still in front knit the next 2 stitches together. This makes a hole in your knitting the right size for a button. Knit the last stitch.

5 Knit the next row, then knit 2 together at the beginning and end of the following row. Knit the remaining 7 stitches in the next row. Decrease by another 2 stitches in the following row so there are 5 stitches left on the marked needle.

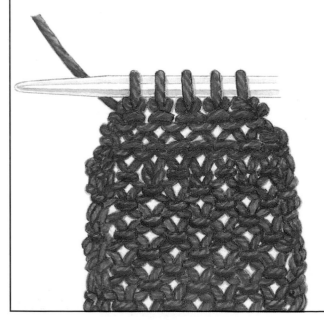

7 With 5 stitches on the unmarked needle, knit the first 2 together. Knit the new stitch (it will be loose) and then knit the last 2 together. Cast off (page 14) the last 3 stitches.

8 Fold the wallet in half. Using yarn and a yarn needle, sew the side seams. Weave in and trim the yarn tails.

9 Turn the wallet right side out. Using the sewing needle and thread, stitch the button in place beneath the buttonhole.

KNIT ON!

● To add a handle to your wallet, knit a skinny strap by casting on 3 or 4 stitches and knitting them in stockinette stitch or garter stitch (page 11) until the strap is the length you want. Sew one end of the strap to each side of the wallet.

● Make a fuzzy wallet using novelty yarn. The seed stitch won't show, so just knit every stitch. Or try combining two yarns for a unique wallet.

● For a cell phone cozy, cast on 7 or 9 stitches and make the cozy as long as it needs to be to fit your phone. Decrease to make the flap, then make a buttonhole as in step 6.

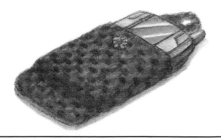

Puffy pillow

For this pillow cover, use two balls of the same color yarn for a solid-color pillow or two different colors for a variegated look.

YOU WILL NEED

- about 64 m (70 yd.) each of 2 balls of fun fur or eyelash novelty yarn
- knitting needles, size 12 mm (U.S. 17)
- a 30 cm (12 in.) pillow form
- a ruler or measuring tape, scissors, a yarn needle

1 Using both yarns at the same time, hold the two ends together as if they were one. Make a slipknot about 150 cm (60 in.) from the end and cast on (page 6) 24 loose stitches. Do not trim the tail.

2 Knit (page 8) every stitch (garter stitch, page 11) until you have a rectangle long enough to cover both sides of the pillow form.

3 Cast off (page 14), leaving a 60 cm (24 in.) tail.

4 Fold the knitting in half. Thread one of the yarn tails into the yarn needle and stitch together one side. Use the other yarn tail to stitch one of the other sides together. Turn the cover right side out, slip in the pillow form and stitch the cover closed. Weave in and trim the yarn tails.

Fuzzy foot mat

Treat your feet to a soft bedside mat that you knitted yourself! Make a Puffy pillow (page 32) to match.

YOU WILL NEED

- about 92 m (100 yd.) of thick, soft chenille yarn
- about 92 m (100 yd.) of fun fur or eyelash novelty yarn
- knitting needles, size 10 mm (U.S. 15)
- a ruler or measuring tape, scissors, a yarn needle

1 Using both yarns at the same time, hold the two ends together as if they were one. Make a slipknot about 150 cm (60 in.) from the end and cast on (page 6) 28 loose stitches.

2 Knit (page 8) every stitch (garter stitch, page 11) until you have about 45 cm (18 in.). If you'd like a longer mat, knit until you almost run out of yarn, then tie the end from a new ball of yarn to the end of the working yarn and continue.

3 Cast off (page 14). Use a yarn needle to weave in the yarn tail, then trim it.

4 See "Knit on!" (page 19) if you'd like to add a fringe to your mat.

Silly slippers

You'll have fun knitting these crazy, cozy slippers. If your foot is quite small, cast on about 14 stitches instead of 18.

YOU WILL NEED

- about 60 m (66 yd.) of chunky weight yarn, with a gauge of about 15 stitches in 10 cm (4 in.)
- about 60 m (66 yd.) of fun fur or eyelash novelty yarn
- knitting needles, size 8 mm (U.S. 11)
- two buttons or beads, or four large sew-on rolly eyes
- a sewing needle and thread to match your yarn
- a ruler or measuring tape, scissors, a yarn needle

1 Measure the length of your bare foot. Subtract about 2.5 cm (1 in.) and make the slippers that length.

2 Using both yarns at the same time, hold the two ends together as if they were one. Make a slipknot about 100 cm (40 in.) from the end and cast on (page 6) 18 stitches. You will have a long yarn tail.

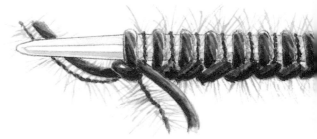

3 Mark the empty needle with a short piece of yarn at the knob end. Knit (page 8) every stitch in every row (garter stitch, page 11). Stop when your knitting is about two-thirds the length of the finished slipper and all the stitches are on the unmarked needle.

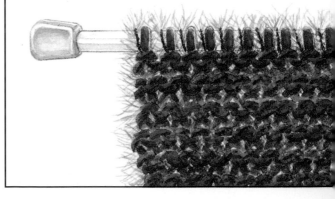

4 Knit one more row, then purl (page 10) the next. Continue knitting and purling (stockinette stitch, page 11) until your slipper is the right length and the stitches are on the unmarked needle.

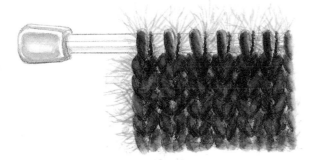

5 Cut the working yarn, leaving a 50 cm (20 in.) tail. Thread it into the yarn needle. Slide the stitches from the knitting needle to the yarn needle and onto the tail, catching all the double loops.

6 With the slipper inside out, pull the yarn tail firmly to gather the stitches into a tight toe circle. Using the yarn needle, stitch this toe circle closed.

7 Stitch together the top of the slipper from the toe to just past the end of the stockinette-stitched area. Finish with a couple of stitches in the same spot, then weave in and trim the yarn tail.

8 Use the other yarn tail to stitch the heel together. Finish with a couple of stitches in the same spot, then weave in and trim the yarn tail.

9 Turn the slipper right side out. Using the sewing needle and thread, stitch a button, bead or a pair of rolly eyes onto the top.

10 Knit another slipper. If the slippers are too loose on your feet, make two braided cords with yarn. Use the yarn needle or your fingers to weave a cord around the top of each slipper opening. Tighten, then tie, the cord into a bow on the top of each foot.

Quick-knit sweater

A sweater usually takes a long time to knit, so you'll be amazed at how soon you're wearing this quick-knit version! It's meant to fit loosely, so don't worry about an exact size.

YOU WILL NEED

- about 600 m (655 yd.) of knitting worsted weight yarn, with a gauge of about 18 stitches in 10 cm (4 in.)
- about 600 m (655 yd.) of chunky weight yarn, with a gauge of about 15 stitches in 10 cm (4 in.)
- knitting needles, size 10 mm (U.S. 15)
- a pencil and paper
- a calculator
- an iron and ironing board
- a ruler or measuring tape, scissors, straight pins, a yarn needle

1   Choose a sweater or sweatshirt that fits you well and use it as a guide for how wide to knit your new sweater. Measure it across the front from underarm to underarm and write down the number you get in centimeters or inches.

2 To figure out how many stitches to cast on, you will need to knit a test swatch as follows:

a) Using both of your yarns at the same time, hold the two ends together as if they were one. Make a slipknot about 65 cm (25 in.) from the end and cast on (page 6) 16 stitches. Mark the knob end of the empty needle with a piece of yarn.

b) Knit the swatch in the stockinette stitch (page 11). After about 10 cm (4 in.) of knitting, and with the stitches on the unmarked needle, loosely cast off (page 14).

c) Without stretching the swatch, pin it flat on an ironing board. With a ruler or measuring tape and straight pins, mark a 10 cm (4 in.) width inside the edges of the swatch. Count every stitch (they look like **V**s), including half stitches, in that width. (You will likely get between 9 and 12 stitches.)

Using the calculator, divide your number of stitches by 10 if you are working in centimeters, or by 4 if you are working in inches. That gives you the number of stitches you knit per centimeter or inch — write it down because you will need it again when you are knitting the neck of your sweater. Multiply the number by the width you wrote down in step 1. (If you end up with a half stitch, round it up.) Add 2 stitches to the number you get. That is how many stitches to cast on to get the width of the front of your sweater. (The back of the sweater will be exactly the same.)

3 Using both yarns at the same time, hold the two ends together as if they were one. Make a slipknot about 190 cm (75 in.) from the end and cast your stitches onto the unmarked needle.

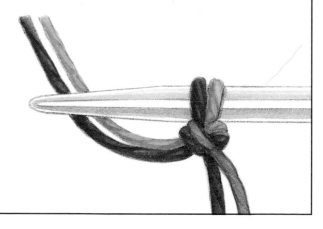

Instructions continue on the next page ☞

4 Knit in stockinette stitch until your sweater is the length you want and all the stitches are on the unmarked needle.

5 To make the neck, you will need to cast off some stitches. To figure out how many, subtract 20 cm (8 in.) from the width of your sweater front. Divide the results by 2, then multiply that number by the number of stitches you knit per centimeter or inch (the number you figured out in step 2 c).

6 Cast off that number of stitches at the beginning of the next row (mark them down as you go, just in case you lose count), then knit the rest of the row.

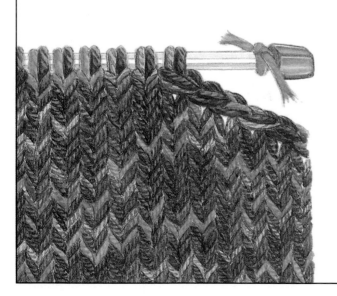

7 At the beginning of the next row, cast off the same number of stitches while purling. Purl the rest of the shortened row.

8 Knit 4 more rows of stockinette stitch to make a rolled neck band. Very loosely cast off the stitches.

9 Make the sweater back the same way, following steps 3 to 8.

10 Without stretching the front of the sweater, pin it, good side down, to the ironing board. You will need to uncurl the sides, but don't pin, press or unroll the neck or bottom. Place a damp pressing cloth on one area at a time and ask an adult to help you press it very gently with a hot, steamy iron. Press the back of the sweater the same way.

11 Using one of the yarns and the yarn needle, stitch the front and back of the sweater together, good sides facing, at the shoulders and at the sides of the neck.

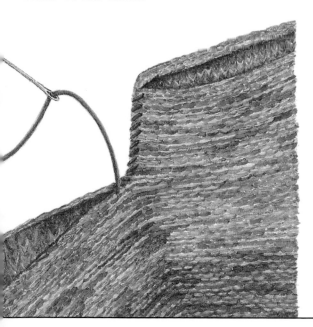

12 For one sleeve, cast 18 stitches onto the unmarked needle. Knit in stockinette stitch until you have 5 cm (2 in.) and the stitches are on the unmarked needle.

13 On the next row, knit two stitches, then increase (page 12) 1 stitch. Knit that row until there are 3 stitches left, increase 1 stitch and knit the last 2 stitches. You should now have 20 stitches.

14 After five more rows of stockinette stitch, and with the stitches on the unmarked needle, increase by one stitch near the beginning and end of the next row, the same as in step 13.

Instructions continue on the next page ☞

15 Keep knitting in stockinette stitch, increasing by 2 stitches every sixth row until your sleeve is long enough or you have 36 stitches. To figure out when your sleeve is long enough, try on your partially finished sweater and hold the sleeve up to the shoulder. Continue knitting the 36 stitches until the sleeve is the right length, then cast off. Make another sleeve exactly the same.

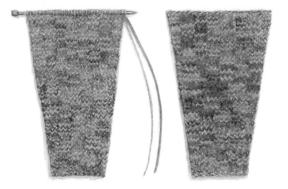

16 See step 10 for how to press the sleeves.

17 Spread out the sweater, good side up. Fold one of the sleeves in half along its widest part and mark the center point with a pin. With the good side down, pin the top of the center of the sleeve to one of the shoulder seams. Stitch it in place as shown. Stitch the other sleeve in place, too.

18 Fold the sweater in half, inside out. Pin, then stitch together one side, starting at the cuff, then up the arm, and down the side to the bottom. Stitch together the other side, too. Remove the pins, then weave in and trim all the yarn ends. Turn the sweater right side out and try it on!

TIP

Since you will be using a number of balls of yarn, you need to keep track of when you get near the end of one. Make sure that you have enough yarn left to complete a row, because you don't want to have a knot on the front of your sweater. Tie the new ball of yarn at the edge before you begin a new row. If you have started a row and run out of yarn, you may need to unknit (page 17) the row, tie on the new ball of yarn at the side edge and continue knitting.